49 DAYS TO THE SUN

Julie Marie Myatt

BROADWAY PLAY PUBLISHING INC
New York
www.broadwayplaypublishing.com
info@broadwayplaypublishing.com

49 DAYS TO THE SUN
© Copyright 2019 Julie Marie Myatt

Cover photo by the author

First edition: January 2019
I S B N: 978-0-88145-810-7

Book design: Marie Donovan
Page make-up: Adobe InDesign
Typeface: Palatino

49 DAYS TO THE SUN was written in Minneapolis in 2001.

CHARACTERS & SETTING

CLYDE
CLYDE'S INNER THOUGHTS, *as told through parenthesis*
MEL
MYRA
SYLVIA
WILL

The Bardo state

The parentheticals are all uttered by an onstage actor. As CLYDE *gets closer to saying good-bye to his body, his speech mixes in form.*

"O nobly-born (Clyde Macey), the time hath now come for thee to seek the Path (in reality). Thy breathing is about to cease. Thy guru hath set thee face to face before with the Clear Light; and now thou art about to experience it in its Reality in the *Bardo* state, wherein all things are like the void and cloudless sky, and the naked spotless intellect is like unto a transparent vacuum without circumference or center. At this moment, know thou thyself; and abide in that state."
The Tibetan Book of the Dead

Day 3

One chair sits on stage. CLYDE *enters confused. Disheveled*

CLYDE: Well. Hell.

He sighs.

I'm not sure where I'm—

He looks around, then keeps walking, off stage.

Day 4

CLYDE *enters, stops.*

CLYDE: Well. Huh.

He sighs.

Maybe.

He looks around, then looks himself over.

Are these the right shoes? My socks aren't clean. My hair is too long. My teeth hurt; I need x-rays. I've got bruises on my arms. This damn scab across my chest. (Fear picks away at it.)

He sighs, holds his heart.

Hell… My privates are still sweaty from that girl— well, who am I kidding—that woman I love. Someday she'll have me. (Just as I've imagined it.) Mark my word. We'll have each other. (In the flesh.)

He adjust his trousers. Sighs again

Shit.

He puts his hand to his forehead, look in the distance.

Maybe I should ask her to marry me… No. No. Too
much. Too much. Not yet. I'll wait until we've kissed.
I'll wait until we've held hands. I'll wait until she sees
me. I'll wait until she's divorced.

He takes a seat. Checks his watch. Smells his breath

Wow. That's not pretty. (Could kill a horse with that.)

*He searches a mint in his pocket. Finds one. Pops it in his
mouth. Picks a hair out of his mouth. [From the mint]*

Damn dog.

He smells his arm pit.

Lord. That's toxic.

Smells himself again, just to make sure.

Jesus. (I'm falling apart.)

He examines his arms. The bruises

You'd think I'd get used to getting knocked around
a bit. But no. Body's got other plans… Every time it
sends out the red flags. The purple hearts. The blue
nuns. All of them telling the world you took a fall.
Screaming: "He stumbled. He's not super man. Two
left feet, this guy. And, he's got the goddamn flesh of a
pansy. The skin of a five year old". (My mother used to
kiss them away.)

He taps the chair.

Shit. (I miss my mother.)

He looks around. Then looks at his shoes again.

I should have splurged on something more stylish.
Comfortable. Maybe some Hush Puppies. No. (Who
wears Hush Puppies?) …These have got Sunday
morning church cheapskate written all over them.
I should have thought about that. I want to be
presentable. I want to impress her. I want to make an
impression. "Start with the shoes. They walk in before
you do, son. Women start with the shoes and work
their way up the man. Remember that". Shit.

He removes his shoes.

(Who wants Billy Graham? Jimmy Baker…a dance with Lawrence Welk?)

CLYDE *is smelling his socks when* MEL *enters with a baby in a baby carrier, strapped to his chest.*

MEL: Morning.

CLYDE *sighs, tosses his socks aside.*

MEL: What?

CLYDE: I thought you said it was just to the left down here.

MEL: It is.

CLYDE: I took every left I could, and nothing.

MEL: Well, maybe I meant the right.

CLYDE: Shit.

MEL: Lovely day though, huh.

CLYDE *looks around.*

CLYDE: I guess.

MEL: Been up since four. Feedings and all.

CLYDE: Uh huh.

MEL: This kid eats more than I do.

CLYDE: What's his name?

MEL: Not sure.

CLYDE: What?

MEL: Well, just hasn't come into his name yet. We can't make heads or tails of this one. Looks like no one we know.

CLYDE: Huh.

MEL: Doesn't even look like himself yet.

CLYDE: I see.

MEL: You look a little banged up there.

CLYDE: Oh. Yeah.

MEL: Bad circulation.

CLYDE: What?

MEL: Bruise easily?

CLYDE: Yes—

MEL: Poor circulation.

CLYDE: I don't—

MEL: My father's side was like that. Awful looking skin. All of them. Always looked like they'd just fallen down a flight of stairs.

CLYDE: Well, I—

MEL: Take niacin.

CLYDE: What?

MEL: Niacin. Vitamin. Works wonders.

He takes bottle out of his pocket and takes a sip.

CLYDE *watches.*

MEL: Man, that's good.

CLYDE: Is it—

MEL: Breast milk. Can't beat it. Sweet stuff.

CLYDE: Seems like you might want to save some for the kid—

MEL: Oh, there's plenty where this came from. Plenty.

CLYDE: So how much further you think I need to go?

MEL: Well…
He wipes his mouth.
Let me think here.
He puts the bottle back in his pocket.
I guess it depends.

CLYDE: Depends on what?

MEL *kisses the top of the baby's head.*

MEL: Depends on how far you're going.

CLYDE *looks around.*

MEL: How far are you going?

CLYDE: How far is it?

MEL: That I don't know.

CLYDE *sighs.*

CLYDE: Could you point me in the right direction?

MEL: I did.

CLYDE: But it was the wrong—

MEL: I tried.

CLYDE: I don't want to wander around here all day.

MEL: Why not? Plenty to see—

CLYDE: I've got things to do. Bills to pay. Appointments to keep. People. Dates.

MEL: I see.

CLYDE: I haven't showered.

MEL: I noticed that.

CLYDE: Did you?

MEL: The breeze. No flowers coming from you.

CLYDE: I know—

MEL: You'll kill a kid with that stench.

CLYDE: I'm sorry—
He sighs.
Shit.

MEL: Tell you what.
He looks around.
Tell you what....

He looks behind and in front of him. To the sides. Squinting for a new way
Come with me.

CLYDE: But you said just back there that you didn't have time—

MEL: Well, things change. I gotta keep moving to keep this kid sleeping now. I can't stop walking. I stop, he wails.

CLYDE: Maybe he wants a name.

MEL: What?

CLYDE: Maybe he's crying for a name.

MEL *starts walking off stage.*

MEL: Doubt it.

CLYDE: Why?

MEL: He's not the type.

CLYDE: How do you know?

MEL *pats the baby.*

MEL: I know.

CLYDE: How?

MEL: I can feel his little heart beating. He could care less about a name.

CLYDE *follows.*

CLYDE: Then why's he cry?

MEL: He's scared.

Day 5

Two chairs on stage
CLYDE *and* MEL; *stop.* CLYDE *sits down. Sighs.*
CLYDE: Shit.

MEL: No one carries a compass anymore, do they.

CLYDE: What?

MEL: The compass. Soon to become obsolete.

CLYDE: You could use one.

MEL *looks around.*

CLYDE: Are you sure that baby's okay?

MEL: Yeah. Why?

CLYDE: He hasn't made a sound in hours.

MEL: We haven't stopped, have we?

CLYDE: No.

MEL: He's happy.

CLYDE: How do you know?

MEL: He's quiet.

CLYDE: He's your kid.

MEL: Indeed.

CLYDE: We passed a lot of forks in these roads.

MEL: These backwoods trails are famous for that.

CLYDE: Really?

MEL: You really should use a bloodhound for this.

CLYDE: I have a dog.

MEL: Oh yeah?

CLYDE: But he's not a bloodhound.

MEL: Won't do much good then.

CLYDE: He's more of a couch dog.

MEL: Why do you have him?

CLYDE: He's good company.

MEL: You city people.

CLYDE: I'm tired. (And lonely.) I should have stayed home. I don't know what I was thinking.

MEL: You were thinking fresh air.

CLYDE: Well—

MEL: Change—

CLYDE: Not—

MEL: Room to roam. Think. Freedom—

CLYDE: No—

MEL: Right?

CLYDE: Exactly.

MEL: No?

CLYDE: I took a wrong turn.

MEL: Huh.

CLYDE: I was following…I was following someone.

MEL: I see.

CLYDE: I got out of the car.

MEL: Yeah.

CLYDE: And I lost her.

(MEL sits down.)

MEL: You lost her?

CLYDE: Out here. She's fast—

MEL: Lost her.

CLYDE: I guess I never had her in the first place.

MEL: Huh.

The baby starts crying.

MEL *immediately stands.*

MEL: Well, there's my cue. Gotta keep moving. Things to see.

CLYDE: Maybe he's hungry.

MEL: Just don't you worry about him.

CLYDE: It's been hours—

MEL: Are you coming?

CLYDE: Now?

MEL: Listen to this kid. He wants action. He sure can belt it out—

CLYDE: No. I can't go any further—

MEL: Why not?

CLYDE: I'm too (too) tired—

MEL: Okay. Suit yourself. Enjoy the sights.

CLYDE *sighs as* MEL *exits. Touches his stomach. Cringes.*

CLYDE: Well, this is brilliant. Fucking wilderness. Sticks and leaves for miles. Birds. Bears. Ridges to climb. Sunshine. Everywhere…I should have worn a hat. Called the Sierra Club. Ranger Rick. "Uh, hello, Green Peace?"…I should have bought some trail mix, something dehydrated…Hell…I should have just talked to her. I should have yelled out. (Am I a stalker?)

He smells himself again. Tears come to his eyes.

Heavens. (I'm profane.)

*(*MYRA *enters, holding her nose.)*

MYRA: Pee Yew. What died?

Holding her breath.

Is that you?

CLYDE: I, I suppose.

MYRA: Wow.

*(*CLYDE *sighs.)*

CLYDE: I know, I know. (I'm ripe.)

MYRA *takes a breath.*

MYRA: Have you seen my husband?

CLYDE: I don't know—

MYRA: He's carrying a baby.

CLYDE: Oh. He just left.

MYRA: Asshole.
She lets out her breath.
Damn it.

CLYDE: Cute kid.

MYRA: What?

CLYDE: Your baby. He's cute.

MYRA: Oh…thank you.
She holds her nose.
He looks just like me.

CLYDE: Yeah?

MYRA: Exactly. Damn that Mel. He's gonna walk that baby to death one of these days. Kid's gonna grow up a pilgrim.

CLYDE: There are worse fates.

MYRA: What?

CLYDE: I don't know. Ditch digger.

MYRA: What do you do?

CLYDE: I, I'm presently unemployed.

MYRA: Uh huh.

CLYDE: Health reasons.

MYRA: Sorry to hear it.

CLYDE: It happens.

MYRA: What are you doing out here? Recovering? Healing? Airing out?

CLYDE: I got lost.

MYRA: Where you trying to go?

CLYDE: Inside a woman.

MYRA: I see. What's her name?

CLYDE: Sylvia.

MYRA: Sylvia?

CLYDE: You know her?

MYRA: Sylvia...

CLYDE: She has a place up here. Somewhere—

MYRA: What's she look like?

CLYDE: Stunning. Brilliant. Hilarious. Charming—

MYRA: Brown hair?

CLYDE: Red.

MYRA: Don't know her. But lots of those people have homes up here now. Under that description. They all look the same to me. Snooty.

CLYDE: She's not—

MYRA: Rich and snooty. Big white teeth. Khaki shorts. Zippers with labels. Baseball hats. Clutching latte coffees and showing off their bright new baby outfits.

CLYDE: Sylvia's not like those people.

MYRA: Sure.

CLYDE: She's exotic and, and—

MYRA: I've gotta find Mel. My tits are about to explode. He gives me no time with my own kid. And I refuse to strap myself to that damn pump just because he's out playing Daniel Boone—

CLYDE: You really should name him.

MYRA *stares at* CLYDE.

MYRA: You ever have a baby?

CLYDE: No—

MYRA: Smelling like that, I don't know what woman—
even that Sylvia bitch—who in their right mind
would—

CLYDE: No need to be nasty—

MYRA: It's no easy task naming a kid.

CLYDE: Well, I imagine—

MYRA: His whole life he's gotta tote that thing around.
Introduce himself. Proclaim himself. Humble himself
to it.

CLYDE: Sure.

MYRA: Think how long it took scientists to name the
planets.

CLYDE: Well—

MYRA: We want our kid to be proud of his name. Fill it
in. A well-fit uniform. Marching forth. Salute the sun.
The warrior of his own word.

CLYDE: Geez.

MYRA: What?

CLYDE: That's a lot of pressure.

MYRA: He's a great kid.

CLYDE: Still—

MYRA: He can handle it.

CLYDE: But until then.

MYRA: Until what?

CLYDE: What do you call him?

MYRA: What ever comes to mind.

CLYDE: Might be confusing—

MYRA: Have you ever had a kid?

CLYDE: No—

MYRA: Then you don't know. It's freedom for him. One day he's "Genius". The next day, "Artist". Another, "Stinky Pants".

CLYDE: Huh.

MYRA: A multitude of men await him.

CLYDE: Huh.

MYRA: Which way did Mel go?

CLYDE: That way.

MYRA: Up there?

CLYDE: Yeah.

MYRA: Damn. Now I'm gonna have to haul these goddamn tits up a goddamn mountain. You give a man a baby, and suddenly he wants to make him a king.

CLYDE: Without a name.

MYRA: Have you ever had a kid?

CLYDE: I told you—

MYRA: Then you don't know. It's painful. Scary. Unknown. *She begins to exit.* A big responsibility—

CLYDE: I imagine—

MYRA: Raising the future.
She exits.

CLYDE *stands. Looks in the distance where she exits. Then in the opposite direction. Sees something familiar. Something exciting.*

CLYDE: Joy of joys! (There is a God in Heaven.)
He waves. Flaps his arms.
Over here! (It's me!)

He jumps up and down.
Sylvia! Sylvia! …SYLVIA!
He runs off stage towards her.
(I'm yours!)

Day 7

CLYDE *stands in the back of the theatre. He looks around, confused. Looks up, around, toward the stage, behind him, above.*

CLYDE: Well. Hell.

Day 9

CLYDE *stands on stage. Looks around.*

CLYDE: Shit.
He wanders off stage, searching.

Day 10

SYLVIA *sits tanning herself. Reading a magazine. Her husband,* WILL *sits beside her, his face hidden by a book. A third chair has been added.*

SYLVIA: You would think that these so-called educated people would have better things to do with their time. Nothing but scandal and trouble, lies and deceit. Sickening really.
She turns the page.
A waste.
She turns another page.
Frivolity abounds.
She turns another page.

Wide-spread consumerism mixed with some phoney
boloney attempt to mask it with yet another spiritual
movement. Efforts to 'expand the meaning of one's
life'. Please. It's nothing but an excuse for another trip
to The Pottery Barn for a new sofa, vase, and rose-
scented "Prosperity" candles.

She stops, riveted.

That *is* a great couch. Wonder what they paid for it.

CLYDE *enters, panting.*

SYLVIA *looks up from her magazine. Smiles at* CLYDE,
*frowns, coughs from the smell of him, then quickly returns
to it.*

*He sits a small distance from the couple. Pretends to be
looking at the nature.*

SYLVIA: I swear, Will, if I had my way with this
country, we'd be using a little more elbow grease and
a lot less massage oil. All this mind/body therapy has
made people into nothing but sniveling cry babies
with yoga mats, plastic Buddhas and acupuncture
needles stuck up their asses. Suddenly people who
never even knew they had chakras are complaining
they're "clogged". Their "chi" is out of whack. Their
dharma is in "utter disarray". I mean it, if I hear
one more reference to Feng Shui, see one more self-
congratulatory sun salutation, or smell one more
sandalwood bath, I'm going to march on up to India
and raise a royal stink. Trek over to Tibet and demand
they stop ringing all those goddamn bells, and stand
up and do something.

CLYDE: (I agree.)

SYLVIA: I mean. Really. They think China's raping their
land? Killing their culture? Well, have a good look
around folks, the good old U S of A is stealing every
sacred practice and cultural icon they can. In the name
of "Spiritual Growth". In the name of "Better Homes

and Gardens". In the name of "Good health". In the
name of "Buy me a ticket to happiness - no, sorry,
make that two. No, hell, make it the ValuPack. Don't
want to run out".

CLYDE: (Uh huh.)

SYLVIA: Pretty soon we'll be selling Dalai Lama quotes
right next to the Hormel Chili and Fruit Loops. You'll
be able to buy a box of Hamburger Helper with mantra
on the back, and jar of mayonnaise with a blessing on
the eggs.

CLYDE: (Yep.)

SYLVIA: It's not that I think we should be kept from
those sacred things. Oh no. Or be denied access to
a more meaningful way to approach life than those
humorless Puritans that settled this land gave us
to chew on or could have ever imagined. I mean,
Lord knows this country and it's native people have
been royally screwed over by all those brow-beating
Christian doctrines. Which, of course, I know are light
years, Light Years, from what the East has always held
to be true. Hell, they got the Occidentalists beat by a
mile. And about a million years. But. But, I do maintain
that once you let this capitalist, consumer-driven,
spiritually lost country, that yes, I know, I call home,
once you let us make your culture, like say, Tibet, the
latest oil field, the Gold Rush, the Diamond Mine,
something very True is ripped from your ancient soil.
The rich soil that understood all these Truths, actually
Understands these Truths and ideas because they've
raised tiny children, comforted the sick and dying
on these expansive, profound beliefs for Centuries,
Centuries we cleverly spent pounding on rocks for
fire and arguing the world was flat…that wise old soil
up there is somehow dishonored and starved simply
by the fact that we in this country want to Use it as

quickly and easily as we use a new shampoo. Because
we want to smell and feel better in the world. Shine
more brightly. Illuminate. Burn. We all just want to
Shine so much more than we do.

CLYDE: I agree! I agree!

SYLVIA *looks at* WILL, *then finally looks at* CLYDE.

SYLVIA: What?

CLYDE: One hundred percent!

SYLVIA: Well...
She gathers herself.
...Anyone in their right mind would.
She smiles and returns to her magazine.
It's just so obvious.

WILL *wakes and moves his book.*

WILL: What's that smell?
He waves the air.
How long did I sleep?

SYLVIA: Were you sleeping?

WILL *checks his watch. Hits it like a stop watch.*

WILL: Half an hour.

SYLVIA: You're getting burned.

WILL: I feel much better now. Needed that nap. Power
naps. They work wonders.

SYLVIA *continues through her magazine.* WILL *stretches.*

WILL: You should try it.

SYLVIA: I am not, and never will be, a napper.

WILL: Your loss. Healthy stuff.

SYLVIA: Time-consuming.

WILL: Most countries understand the mid-day snooze. Spain shuts down. Mexico has the siesta. China takes an hour—

SYLVIA: Hours in the day, lost. Could be better used—

CLYDE: (I haven't taken a nap since I was five.)

SYLVIA: Making lists.

WILL: People need to rest.

CLYDE: (I haven't slept since I was eighteen.)

SYLVIA *hears* CLYDE's *mumbling. Stops. Then continues.*

SYLVIA: Vacation is enough rest for me. It's all that I can handle. Being idle. I miss—

CLYDE: Where're you from?

WILL *finally takes notice of* CLYDE.

WILL: Afternoon.

CLYDE *looks up at the sky.*

CLYDE: (So it is.) Hello.

WILL: We're from the City. You?

CLYDE: Oh. Same.

WILL: Really? What part?

CLYDE: I'm not really from there. (Is anyone?) North Carolina—

WILL: Sylvia's from Canada.

CLYDE: Really? (Wow.)

SYLVIA: It's not that exotic.

CLYDE: Are you French—

SYLVIA: Not exotic at all.

WILL: You look familiar.

CLYDE: Do I?

WILL: You work the Market?

CLYDE: Uh. No.

WILL: Lawyer?

CLYDE: No.

WILL: Shrink?

CLYDE: No.

WILL: I swear, I—

CLYDE: Nope.

WILL: Hmm.

SYLVIA: He works in the coffee store.

WILL: Maybe—

CLYDE: No.

SYLVIA: Yes—

CLYDE: Impossible.

SYLVIA: I've seen you—

CLYDE: No. (You noticed me too?) No—

SYLVIA: Will, you're legs are burned. Put some sunscreen on or something—

WILL: You up here on vacation?

CLYDE: Yes. (So to speak.)

WILL: I love this country. Fresh and wild.

CLYDE: It's fresh alright. (Vast and full of strangers. Babies.)

SYLVIA: It's dull.

WILL: Lots of kids around. Big baby boom going on. Have you noticed that?

CLYDE: I guess—

WILL: Everyone's packing a little one. I would be too, but Sylvia here doesn't believe in them.

SYLVIA: World's got plenty of people in it.

WILL: See?

SYLVIA: We'll go to China if we want a baby.

WILL: They drown the girls.

SYLVIA: Someone's got to save them.

CLYDE: My goodness. (I love you.)

SYLVIA: What?

CLYDE: That's noble. To save them.

SYLVIA: It's a basic human response.

WILL: Still would've like to pass on my genes though.

SYLVIA: Egotism.

WILL: My grandfather was brilliant.

SYLVIA: He invented "Krazy Glue".

WILL: Powerful stuff.

SYLVIA: Saving coffee mugs across the country.

WILL: Men can hang from buildings on it—

SYLVIA: But it can't keep a Chinese girl from getting her face shoved down a river.

WILL *is silent.* CLYDE *admires* SYLVIA. WILL *picks up his book.*

WILL: Well then. If you'll excuse me…

CLYDE: Clyde.

WILL: Clyde. Nice to meet you. I'm going inside. It seems I need more S P F. Maybe I'll make a sport shake. My protein feels low.

CLYDE: See you around.

WILL *catches a whiff of* CLYDE.

WILL: Have, have you been in the lake?

CLYDE: Not yet.

WILL: Do try it. It, it, it has a refreshing, cleansing effect.

CLYDE: I will.

WILL *glances at* SYLVIA *and exits. She returns to her magazine, scratches her long leg.* CLYDE *watches her.*

CLYDE: You know, you know…you do look a bit familiar as well.

SYLVIA: You've been following me for six months. Don't play coy with me.

CLYDE: Coy? (She's on to me!)

SYLVIA: I heard that. I am on to you. It's a long way to come for a crush.

CLYDE: Crush? (Am I that obvious?)

SYLVIA: I saw you behind us on the road. Where'd you learn to drive?

CLYDE: I didn't.

SYLVIA: Obviously.

CLYDE *touches his stomach.*

CLYDE: I wrecked it.

SYLVIA *puts the magazine aside, concerned.*

SYLVIA: That was *your* car?

CLYDE: I didn't own it—

SYLVIA: In that tree?

CLYDE: Was it a tree? I thought it was a pole—

SYLVIA: No one could have walked out of that car.

CLYDE: Well—

SYLVIA: There was nothing left. Mangled and wrapped around it like that.

CLYDE: I didn't see it coming. (Does anyone?)

SYLVIA: I guess not.

CLYDE: I was distracted. (I'm faint just looking at you.)

SYLVIA: Have you been checked out? By doctors?

CLYDE: No. (You're killing me.)

SYLVIA: You should be.

CLYDE: I know. (I'm already dead.)

SYLVIA: Jesus Christ. I didn't know that was your car.

CLYDE: Yep.

SYLVIA: Will and I just passed it yesterday. I vomited on the spot. They were peeling it off the—

CLYDE: Windy roads up here.

SYLVIA: Yes.

CLYDE: Lots of turns.

SYLVIA: I feel horrible.

CLYDE: I would have showered, but there's been no way—

SYLVIA: Because of me.

CLYDE: Well—

SYLVIA: I'll admit, I'm flattered. I've never been followed. For so long—

CLYDE: (Stalked?)

SYLVIA: Are you stalking me?

CLYDE: No.

SYLVIA: You poor thing.

CLYDE: No—

SYLVIA: How very pathetic.

MEL *enters with the baby, and waves his hand in front of his nose.*

MEL: I see you found her.

CLYDE: Yes, thank you, now please leave us—

MEL: Mel.

MEL *shakes* SYLVIA's *hand. Glances behind them.*

MEL: Ah. You bought the Cooper place.

SYLVIA: Yes.

MEL: Nice bit of land.

SYLVIA: My husband thinks so.

MEL: Lake side. Spectacular views—

SYLVIA: Terribly overpriced.

MEL: Well, you folks seem to want a piece of country life. The Great Divide. I guess you're gonna have to pay for it, aren't you?

SYLVIA: "You folks"?

MEL: Come now.

He adjusts the baby in the carrier.

You know who you are.

SYLVIA *stands. She is a glorious, tall creature.*

CLYDE: Don't you need to keep moving, mister? (For Christ's sake, you're stealing my fire!)

MEL: You are a lovely woman, aren't you?

To CLYDE.

I'd follow her.

SYLVIA: You seem to think I belong to some sort of "type". Some sort of "definition" of "city slicker". "Outsiders" with enough money to feed four if not five third world countries if they put their heads and wallets together, that you see buying up, jacking up, and overrunning your quiet, "natural" once remote, once peaceful surroundings. Your paradise. Your heaven. Your garden. Your "home".

MEL: Uh huh.

SYLVIA: Guilty as charged.

MEL: Glad we got that straight.

SYLVIA *holds out her hand.*

SYLVIA: Sylvia. Nice to meet you.

MEL: Pleasure's mine.

SYLVIA: So then, to be clear, you're that slap-happy local country backwoods bumpkin, who raises his kids on hominy, fat back and your pappy's anecdotes, who shoots bottles and cans in the back yard, throws his trash next to the family's rusty Buick, but can sing and stomp his feet like a pro if the right fiddle or banjo's playing.

MEL *gives* SYLVIA *another sly grin.*

MEL: The car's on cinder blocks?

SYLVIA: Of course. But of course—

MEL: I don't own a car.

MYRA *enters, exhausted and pissed.*

MYRA: Goddamn it, Mel. Give me that kid.

MEL: Hey baby.

MYRA *is not pleased to see* MEL *flirting with* SYLVIA.

MYRA: Don't hey baby me. Poor kid would be better off in Outward Bound than with you.

MEL: He loves it.

MYRA: Hand him over. I'd like a little time with my own son, Mel. Just a little time.

MEL *unstraps the baby.*

MYRA *takes him from* MEL *and takes a seat in one of the chairs. She opens her shirt.*

CLYDE *stares.*

MYRA: Do you mind?

CLYDE: Oh. No. Not at all. (Oh dear mother, where are you now?)

SYLVIA: What's his name?

CLYDE: Don't ask.

MYRA *gives* SYLVIA *a dirty look.*

MEL: It's, it's yet to be decided.

They all watch the baby nurse.

Day 12

MYRA *burps the baby and they are still staring.* WILL *has now joined the other four in the staring.*

WILL *checks his watch. Hits it again like a stop watch.*

WILL: Two hours.

MEL: On the dot.

WILL: I didn't know a baby could drink that much.

MYRA: He will when he's out with one of the last Mohicans.

MEL: Adventure never hurt a kid.

MYRA: He'll be jumping box cars by the time he's four.

MEL: He'll know the world.

MYRA: Up on Everest by ten.

MEL: Straight to the top.

MYRA: The South Pole by seventeen.

MEL: Down but not out.

MYRA: Quam by twenty.

MEL: Proud pirate of the Pacific.

MYRA: "Good-bye mother".

MEL: "Hello hero".

MYRA *sneaks a smile as she hands the baby back to* MEL. *He straps him back in the pack.*

CLYDE: Without a name.

MYRA: Have you ever had a—

CLYDE: How will he ever be remembered if—

WILL: Now that is a good looking baby. Sylvia here won't partake—

SYLVIA: Remember that car?

WILL: The wreck?

SYLVIA: That was him.

WILL: Who?

SYLVIA: This guy.

WILL: Clyde?

SYLVIA: Yes.

WILL: Impossible.

SYLVIA: In the flesh.

MEL: That man's gone.

CLYDE: No. I'm here. (If you could just let me be alone with her.)

MEL: No…

CLYDE: Yes.

MEL: The steering wheel went through the guy's gut.

CLYDE: And it did not feel good. (I've got the stomach ache to prove it.)

MEL: His head hit the windshield.

CLYDE: And it was not pleasant. (I'm still seeing stars.)

SYLVIA: He hasn't seen a doctor. Though who could blame him really. The hospitals, health care, the H M O's as they are—

MYRA: The next hospital's twenty miles—

CLYDE: I'm fine. (Love struck but—)

MEL: That wreck was what, ten days ago now?

CLYDE: Twelve. (But who's counting.)

MEL: Jesus.

They all stare at CLYDE *in amazement. He smiles.*

CLYDE: I'm fine.

They continue staring. CLYDE *smiles some more.*

SYLVIA: You have a place to stay?

CLYDE: Pardon?

SYLVIA: A place to stay?

CLYDE: Oh. No. (Take me in your arms.)

WILL: We've got a guest room. Hell, we've got four of them.

MEL: Must be nice.

SYLVIA: Don't start.

MEL: It's your money.

WILL: This place was a steal.

MEL: Don't tell Cooper.

WILL: We paid cash.

SYLVIA: I think you should get some rest, Clyde.

CLYDE: I'm fine. (Hold me.)

SYLVIA: It's decided. You're staying with us.

CLYDE: I wouldn't want to put you out. (Just your husband.)

WILL: Truth be told, we're bored to death up here.

MEL: Of course you are.

SYLVIA: I know a little about medicine.

WILL: Her first husband was a doctor.

SYLVIA: I put him through Med school.

The baby cries.

MEL: That's my bugle. Kid's ready to go.

MYRA: But the sun's going down.

MEL: Tell that to him.

MYRA: He's bound to be restless, Mel. Obsessive. You're going to make him into—

MEL: That's the very nature of Genius, honey.

MYRA: Oh? …Is it?

MEL *and* MYRA *both smile as they exit together.*

SYLVIA: I'm going to need a few things. Yes. I'm going to need to bring out all the stops. Hmm… Let me think…don't worry, I'm good at this…please, Clyde, follow me.

WILL: I insist.

SYLVIA: I'll have you better in days.
She exits.

CLYDE: (I don't mind if it takes the rest of my life.)

WILL: What's that?

CLYDE: Thank you.

WILL: Hey, my Sylvia's got a weakness for the sick. I was battling prostate cancer when she met me.

CLYDE: You don't say?

WILL: Been in remission ever since.

CLYDE: She's sure something. (She's mine.)

WILL: All fire that woman. All fire.

CLYDE *and* WILL *exit.*

Day 15

CLYDE *stands naked in small tub, his arms in the air. A chair beside him.*

SYLVIA *walks around him in circle, wrapping a large bandage around his stomach.*

SYLVIA: Too tight?

CLYDE: No. (Just right.)

CLYDE *smiles as* SYLVIA *continues to walk around him.*

Day 18

CLYDE *stands in the same tub. Arms in the air.*

SYLVIA *walks in the opposite direction, unwrapping the bandages. They are soaked with blood.*

SYLVIA: Don't worry. Just a minor set back.

CLYDE: No harm done.

SYLVIA: I've got it all under control.

CLYDE: (I'm all yours.)

Day 20

CLYDE *lies on a flat bed, the three chairs surrounding him. He looks worse—bruises are darker and his eyes are more sunken.*

Incense are burning. [It is the beginning of a small shrine that builds beside the bed through out the rest of the play.]

SYLVIA *enters with a tray and a hot pot of tea.*

SYLVIA: Okay. Here it is. This is the trick.

CLYDE: You're too kind.

SYLVIA: Chinese secret. Beetles and tree bark—

CLYDE: (I think I already have some tree bark stuck in my gut. A woodpecker too. Eggs. A small nest.)

SYLVIA: Does wonders.

CLYDE: I'm all for Wonders.

SYLVIA: We're just going to sit you up a bit, huh?

CLYDE: I'd like that. (To gaze in your eyes.)

CLYDE *sits up and* SYLVIA *offers the tea.*

SYLVIA: There we are.

CLYDE *tastes the tea. It's horrible.*

CLYDE: *Sings* "Wonders of wonders…"

CLYDE & SYLVIA: *Sing together* "Miracles, miracles…"

Silence. SYLVIA *studies* CLYDE.

SYLVIA: How old are you?

CLYDE: Thirty-six. (But I'm mature for my age. Wise beyond my—)

SYLVIA: I would have guessed that.
She touches his forehead.
Just a few lines on your face. Around your eyes. No more. A gray hair or two. But still you're boyish.
She removes her hand.

CLYDE: (Touch me again.)

SYLVIA: You shouldn't have followed me.

CLYDE: Maybe. (Please touch me—)

SYLVIA: This wouldn't have happened. You'd still be making coffee for people.

CLYDE: Sure. (God help me.)

SYLVIA: Every time I'd walk in that store, I knew you were watching.

CLYDE: Well, I—

SYLVIA: Eavesdropping on my conversations.

CLYDE: They were fascinating. Alive with vision—

SYLVIA: Studying me.

CLYDE: It's a small store. (You're a big woman.)

SYLVIA: I knew you were unhappy.

CLYDE: Really?

SYLVIA: Weren't you?

CLYDE: How?

SYLVIA: Your apron was always dirty. And wrinkled. Your hair messy. You looked pained. Drained of sleep. Food.

CLYDE: Well...yes. I guess so. (Miserable.)

SYLVIA: Why?

CLYDE: Besides the fact that I'm thirty-six and still working in a coffee shop with sixteen year olds?

SYLVIA: No harm in that—

CLYDE: Making cappuccinos for my peers instead of conversation? Starved for some recognition that I exist outside my humble occupation? My apron?

SYLVIA: Ever been someone's wife?

CLYDE: That I am more than meets the eye? (And too much of a coward to approach you and myself maybe and all I really want from my life is someone to talk to all day long and someone to love the whole night through. All else seems meaningless to me. I strive for nothing but that and yet it escapes me. Why does it escape me—)

SYLVIA: And?

CLYDE: I used to be different.

SYLVIA: How?

CLYDE: I was taller.

SYLVIA: Really—

CLYDE: Light-hearted. Brave. (Maybe. Maybe once. I think once I was. As a boy. I set out on foot—)

SYLVIA: What happened?

CLYDE *pushes a smile.*

CLYDE: I fell someplace. Tripped. Lost my stride. (Someone stole my shoes. My wallet. Took a bat to my face. My boyhood—)

SYLVIA: But this. You. Following me.

CLYDE: Yes. I know. Crazy. (But I had to. Don't you see? For one moment I was new. Driving up here. All courage. Driving. Speeding. Racing. Turning. To you. Please—)

SYLVIA *begins to touch* CLYDE's *stomach.*

SYLVIA: And this. Gash. I'm afraid it's too deep. You've lost. You're—

CLYDE: Heart is wide open. (Save me. Make me brave again.)

WILL *enters in sweaty running clothes. Stopping his watch.*

WILL: One full hour. Great work-out. Everything is burning. Muscles I didn't even know I had. On fire. I love this kind pain. Wow. Man, what a beautiful day. The sun is everywhere. Gorgeous. Great to be alive and kicking.

SYLVIA *passes* WILL *a glance.*

WILL: Who wants to go for a swim? I think I can push myself a little harder—

SYLVIA: You go.

WILL: Hate to swim alone. Why don't you two throw on your suits and join me?

SYLVIA: Not today.

WILL: No time like the present. C'mon, Clyde. You could use a dip. Clean off the old—

SYLVIA: Go ahead.

WILL *pulls* SYLVIA *off to the side.*

WILL: I think it might do him some good.

SYLVIA: He can barely stand.

WILL *smiles at* CLYDE.

WILL: He stinks.

SYLVIA: He swallowed his windshield.

WILL: We should get a real doctor.

SYLVIA: It's too late.

WILL: What do you mean, too late?

WILL *smiles at* CLYDE *again.* CLYDE *smiles back.*

Silence.

WILL: Are we going to let him do that *here*?

SYLVIA: Can we stop it?

WILL: But what about his family? Shouldn't we call someone? His parents? Brothers? Sisters? Someone he knows? Cares? Will come get him—

SYLVIA: None.

WILL: No kin?

SYLVIA: None.

WILL: Heavens.
Silence.
How long do you think it's going to take?

SYLVIA: I'm not sure—

WILL: My goodness.
He looks at his watch.

Well. I guess I should feel sad all the sudden.

SYLVIA: Yes.

WILL: What should I do?

SYLVIA: Be kind.

WILL: Yes. I can do that.

SYLVIA: Sing him songs.

WILL: I do have a good voice.

SYLVIA: Let me be with him.

WILL: What?

SYLVIA: Alone.

WILL: What for?

SYLVIA: He needs help.

WILL: Of course, but—

SYLVIA: Guidance.

WILL: Well—

SYLVIA: Love.

WILL: What kind?

SYLVIA: What?

WILL: Love?

SYLVIA: Go swim.

WILL: Sylvia?

SYLVIA: It there only one?

WILL: What?

SYLVIA: Kind?

WILL: Of?

SYLVIA: He's dying.

WILL: Love?—

CLYDE: I just want to say, I really do appreciate this.

Silence.

WILL: No problem.

CLYDE: Funny. Isn't it? One minute you're driving
down the road, singing at the top of your lungs, the
world at your feet, and the next thing you know,
you're convalescing in the guest room of strangers.
(Was this meant to be?)

WILL: Like I said, we got nothing but time up here.
If it weren't for you, Sylvia would be scratching the
walls, sending angry letters to editors, making lists for
improving next year's fund raisers, planning a cultural
revolution.

SYLVIA: Someone's got to do it.

WILL: Instead, I get to some real R & R, and she gets to
play doctor.

SYLVIA: I'm not playing—

WILL: You, Clyde, are our perfect vacation.

CLYDE: Thank you. (Let me have her.)

WILL: Who needs Waikiki when you've got an invalid
in the house.

SYLVIA: Will—

WILL: Better to attend the dying than nurture the
living—

SYLVIA: Will!

WILL: Fix the broken, then notice the man beside you—

SYLVIA: Will you—

WILL: Yes?

SYLVIA: Go. Swim.

WILL: Yes, dear.

CLYDE: Do a few strokes for me. (I prefer breast.)

WILL *checks his watch.*

WILL: I guess I'll go swim. Try not to drown myself.
He exits.

CLYDE: Good man, your husband. (I wouldn't have married him, but—)
He lies down.

SYLVIA: Are you hungry?

CLYDE: No.

SYLVIA: Are you cold?

CLYDE: No.

SYLVIA: You look a little scared.

CLYDE: (Do I?)

SYLVIA: You're not scared, are you?

CLYDE: No.

SYLVIA: No? Good. No reason to be—

CLYDE: Of course not. (I'm terrified.)

Day 22

SYLVIA *sits alone in a corner of the stage, searching through a stack of books: the Bible, Tibetan Books, Chinese Medicine, Western medicine, Inspirational books, Self-Help manuals, The New York Times, books on death, books on birth, books on gardening, books on astronomy, astrology, books on the power of books, and one very large dictionary. She takes notes.*

CLYDE *enters naked and full of energy.*

CLYDE: Look! Hey! Ho!

(SYLVIA *looks up from her notes.*)

CLYDE: No need to worry. No need to fret. I feel fantastic. See. Ten fingers and toes. All in working order now. See. You did it—
He does a little dance—
(I am your miracle.)
He begins to urinate on himself. He realizes he has no control over it.

SYLVIA *begins to get up, and* CLYDE *holds his hand out for her to stay. He quickly exits. She returns to her notes.*

Day 23

CLYDE *sits under blankets, the chairs surrounding him.*

WILL *sits beside him, playing the guitar, singing.*

WILL: "Hey Mr Tambourine Man, play a song for me..."
He forgets the lyrics. Stops.
How's the rest of that go?

CLYDE: I'm not sure. (I hate folk music.)

WILL: I was in folk group in college. Kind of a Peter, Paul, and Mary thing. We called ourselves, Will, Honor, and Pride. I was Will, of course.

CLYDE: Sure.

WILL: Some people thought I was a dead ringer for Bob Dylan.

CLYDE: Really?

WILL: It was the girls mostly. They'll do anything to get close to a musician.

CLYDE: Right.

WILL: How're you feeling?

CLYDE: Fine.

WILL: Not too hot? Need more shade?

CLYDE: No.

Silence.

WILL: You wanna see my muscles?
He flexes.
I've got some impressive definition happening here—

CLYDE: Not particularly.

Silence.

WILL: Feels good out here, doesn't it? A little air in the old lungs?

CLYDE: (I'm freezing.) Where's Sylvia?

WILL: Taking a nap. Of all things. I took a picture to record it. A day in history.

CLYDE: Oh.

WILL: She must be dead tired for that to happen.

CLYDE: I see.

WILL: What do you two talk about all night?

CLYDE: I don't know. (Everything.)

WILL: The woman can talk. Can't she?

CLYDE: Yes. (She asks about me. *Me.*)

WILL: I wish she could feel as much as she could talk.

CLYDE: What—

WILL *checks his watch.*

WILL: Forty-five minutes. She must be exhausted.

MEL *enters with the baby on his chest.*

MEL: I thought I heard music.

WILL: You sing?

MEL: Not out loud.

WILL: Good for the soul. Adds years to your life—

MEL: Better left to the birds.

WILL *puts down the guitar.*

WILL: How's that baby?

MEL: Excellent. Gained a pound.

WILL *stands and stares at the baby.*

WILL: What's his name again?

MEL: He doesn't have one.

WILL: What?

MEL: We don't know yet.

WILL: Try Will. Will works for me.

MEL: I imagine it does.

WILL: Can I hold him?

MEL *looks* WILL *over, unsure.*

WILL *checks his watch.*

WILL: Five minutes. Just let me hold him for five minutes.

MEL: Don't wake him.

WILL: I won't.

MEL *looks* WILL *over.*

WILL: I won't.

MEL *hands the baby to* WILL.

WILL: Oh my.

MEL: He weighs more than you think.

WILL: About the same as a sack of California oranges.

MEL: About.

WILL: Huh.

He can't help but smile at the baby.

Makes my heart hurt.

MEL: I know.

WILL: Makes me want so much.

MEL: I know.

WILL'*s smile slowly fades. He hands the baby back to* MEL.

MEL: Your five minutes isn't up yet—

WILL: I can't take it.

MEL: What?

WILL: All the possibilities.

MEL *adjusts the baby in his pack.*

WILL: If you'll excuse me…
He quickly exits.

MEL: He's an odd one.

CLYDE: Bored, I think. (He doesn't deserve her.)

MEL: All that money and no where to go. Cry me a river.
He looks CLYDE *over.*
How're you feeling?

CLYDE: Fine.

MEL: You need anything?

CLYDE: No. (Well—)

MEL: Where's your woman?

CLYDE: Sleeping.

MEL: You get her in the sack yet?

CLYDE: Yes.

MEL: Well done—

CLYDE: But we were just talking. (I wanted to undress her, but—)

MEL: All the way up a mountain, into a tree, down a dark path, up a forest, up a ridge, up another ridge, plus who knows how many inclines, just to talk. You city folks.

CLYDE: I wasn't raised in the city.

MEL: No?

CLYDE: No.

MEL: Then what happened to you?

CLYDE: I don't know. (I ran from home. Lost my accent. Tried to change my name. It didn't work.)

MEL: You ashamed of your past?

CLYDE: No. (Yes. I don't know. Maybe.)

MEL: You sure? Doesn't sound like it.

CLYDE: Oh?

MEL: You mumble a lot.

CLYDE: Habit. (Habit.)

MEL: Where's your family?

CLYDE: Dead. (Buried on the side of a mountain.)

MEL: You miss them?

CLYDE: Yes. (Most of the time.)

MEL: Well, I miss my family too. Myra and I are pretty much on our own. But, I guess we like it that way. I guess we do. I know Myra does.

CLYDE: Yeah?

MEL: She's a private woman. I'm a grumpy old man. We both need space. Lots of space. The less hassle, the less boloney the better. We need quiet.

CLYDE: You've got plenty of that.

MEL: Oh, we've got forever up here. This kid's got it all.

CLYDE: No name, but—

MEL: Birds and sky and meadows that run for miles. Earth and expanse. He'll know who he is.

CLYDE: How can you be sure?

MEL: I'm gonna show him.

The baby cries.

MEL: *To the baby:* Okay. We're going.

CLYDE: Do you work?

MEL: What?

CLYDE: Do you have any kind of job?

MEL: Why?

CLYDE: How do you support yourself?

MEL: Why?

He takes out the bottle. Takes a swig of breast milk

CLYDE: I don't know. Just curious—

MEL: This is it. Right here.

CLYDE: What?

MEL: Him.

CLYDE: Really?

MEL: He's it.

CLYDE: Huh.

MEL: 24/7.

CLYDE: Walking the baby?

MEL: Raising my son.

CLYDE: Sounds endless. (Give me that bottle. I want to taste that.) You don't make a living?

MEL: This is what I do.

He exits.

CLYDE *is left alone on stage. Under his blankets.*

CLYDE: Is this what I do?

He looks around. Tries to get up. He's too weak.

Is this who I am?

He looks at his stomach, leans back, shades his face from the sun.

Endless?

He moves his hand, squints to the sun.

Who?

Day 24

SYLVIA *wears sunglasses and smokes a cigarette, staring into the distance, looking out at the mountain. She runs prayer beads through her fingers. She quickly hides the beads when* MYRA *enters with a bag of groceries.*

SYLVIA: Shopping, huh?

MYRA: Damn prices keep getting higher and higher. Organic this. French that. Italian sent. Who the hell needs imported tomatoes? What's wrong with American tomatoes?

SYLVIA: Not as flavorful.

MYRA: Says who?

SYLVIA: You can taste the difference.

MYRA: If you pay enough for it, I guess you're gonna tell yourself that...aren't you?

Silence.

SYLVIA: I don't eat tomatoes.

Silence.

MYRA: How's that man doing?

SYLVIA: Okay, I guess.
She puts out the cigarette.
For dead.

MYRA *nods, adjust the groceries to the other hip like a mother would a child.*

SYLVIA: How's the baby?

MYRA: Excellent, thank you. When I see him—

SYLVIA: Off with his father?

MYRA: You'd think I'd hatched Jesus.

(SYLVIA laughs. MYRA doesn't.)

MYRA: You never know.

SYLVIA: I guess not.

MYRA *adjust her hair.*

SYLVIA: Have you found a name yet?

MYRA: It's not as easy as you—

SYLVIA: Well, I'm sure you will think of something. There's a million kids being born on this shrinking planet and named by the goddamn minute. Something clever and long, or short and pithy. Population skyrocketing beyond belief, and still people are convinced they gotta bring a baby into the world. Gotta bring another mouth to feed. Crime is on the rise, disease and depression, terrorism lurks in every corner of the land, and still, Johnny jump-ups, spinning bunny mobiles and tiny Osh Kosh overalls remain on the minds of the masses.

MYRA: You got a better idea?

SYLVIA: Civil service. Homeless shelters. Feeding the poor—

MYRA: You get much pleasure out of singing a medal to sleep at night?

SYLVIA: Beats watching my child suffer plague, pollution, fear, war, upheaval, disappointment, mental illness, hunger maybe—

MYRA: Who says he—

SYLVIA: She—

MYRA: Won't rise above all the gutters like the rest of us? Enjoy the grass. Sunlight. Italian tomatoes. Cakes. Become the next great—
She stops and looks at SYLVIA.
When you lose her?

SYLVIA: What?

MYRA: Your daughter.

SYLVIA: I didn't.

MYRA: No?

SYLVIA: Fortunately I don't see childbirth as my responsibility as a woman. My cross to bear, speaking of Jesus. No. I've got enough on my plate. More than enough. A woman with my kind of lifestyle, my commitments to—

MYRA: You're sterile, aren't you?

SYLVIA: What?

MYRA: Can't have children?

SYLVIA: I'm not sure that's your business.

MYRA *takes an apple out of the bag. Takes a bite.*

MYRA: Maybe not.

SYLVIA: And I don't see what difference it makes. You can't argue with the population count—

MYRA: It would make a big difference if you had a kid.

SYLVIA *laughs.*

SYLVIA: Please. Save it. I've endured more than my share of pacifier pushing, diaper thumping and cradle cooing than I care to—

MYRA: I just pushed my son out of me at forty-five.

SYLVIA *removes her sunglasses.*

SYLVIA: And?

MYRA: I've been in your shoes.

SYLVIA: I don't think so—

MYRA: But that—

SYLVIA: My shoes are hard to fill—

MYRA: Miracle of birth—

SYLVIA: Please—

MYRA: You can't argue with that.

SYLVIA: Oh, I think I can. I can argue with just about anything. Try me—

MYRA: No—

SYLVIA: I've made patrons and corporations hand over millions, made grown men cry, made—

MYRA: Not until you've felt your belly grow…and screamed the child of your lover straight into his shaking arms. Held that fresh life—that bloody new hope—in your own hands and—

SYLVIA: Stop.

MYRA: Not until you've held—

SYLVIA: I said stop.

MYRA *keeps eating the apple.*

MYRA: I'm sorry…

She begins to exit.

But you can't argue with that, woman.

SYLVIA *watches* MYRA *go. Pushes a laugh. Puts on her sunglasses and takes out her prayer beads.*

Day 27

SYLVIA *sits reading from the* Tibetan Book of the Dead *to* CLYDE *as he sleeps.*

SYLVIA: "O nobly-born, the possessor of that sort of body will see places familiarly known on the earth-plane and relatives there as one seeth another in dreams. Thou seest thy relatives and connections and speakest to them, but receivest no reply. Then, seeing them and thy family weeping, though thinkest, 'I am dead! What shall I do?' and feelest great misery, just like a fish cast out of water on red-hot embers. Such misery thou wilt be experiencing at present. But feeling miserable will avail thee to nothing now. If thou has a divine guru, pray to him. Pray to the Tutelary Deity, the Compassionate One. Even though thou feelest attachment to thy relatives and connections, it will do thee no good. So be not attached. Pray to the Compassionate Lord; thou shalt have nought of sorrow, or of terror, or of awe."

WILL *enters, hits his watch.*

SYLVIA *stops reading, hides the book.*

WILL: Time for bed.

SYLVIA: You go.

WILL *approaches* SYLVIA *and touches her shoulder.*

WILL: Sylvia—

(WILL *tries to kiss* SYLVIA.)

SYLVIA: I'm busy.

WILL *pulls away. He exits.*

CLYDE *quickly wakes. And smiles.*

Day 29

CLYDE: (A weeper.)

CLYDE *sits up in a chair, talking.* SYLVIA *listens.*

SYLVIA: A weeper?

CLYDE: (There are these things, so many things, that move me that I can't explain.)

SYLVIA: Like what?

CLYDE: (Everything. Everything really. I'm struck. The world. It wounds me.)

SYLVIA: Let it—

CLYDE: (It suddenly all becomes so overwhelming. Glaring. Life. People. Small moments. Changing everything. When I catch those moments, with me, through other people, I, I can't see straight. My eyes are full of tears. There's always so many tears. I can't stop them. As if every image I see is accompanied by rain. By clouds. By approaching thunder. A wrath of emotion that I can't control. I am a child—)

SYLVIA: And?

CLYDE: (I see love I can't have.)

SYLVIA: What?

CLYDE: (I think that's what starts it. Women. Couples. Children. So many children. And hunger. And unhappiness. And desire. Unending desire...I can't give the love anybody needs. Or get it. Maybe I just want to get it. I think I just want to get it.)

SYLVIA: What would you do with it?

CLYDE: (Grab it. Hold it. Hold it until I've had enough.)

SYLVIA: You think that's possible?

CLYDE: (No.)
(And that's what makes me cry all the more. It will never be enough. That's what tortures me. Do you think it tortures everyone?)

SYLVIA: Yes.

CLYDE: Really?

SYLVIA: I would imagine.

CLYDE: (Why is it so hard?)

SYLVIA: I'm not sure.

CLYDE: (It should be simple.)

SYLVIA: I know—

CLYDE: (Like breathing… People love dogs easily. Babies. Movie stars. Food. Sports. But each other? People keep each other at bay. I don't understand that…I feel as if my whole life I've been kept at bay from someone.)

SYLVIA: Who?

CLYDE: (The people I try to grab. And hold.)

SYLVIA: What happens?

CLYDE: (My grip is too tight. I try and soak them dry. Drink their eyes.)

SYLVIA: Habit.

CLYDE: (I want their mouth in mine. I want to taste their thoughts. I want to put their chest inside mine. Our ribs tangled. Hearts shoved up against each other. Whispering. Like two people in the middle of a crowded subway. Flirting. Pressed together and moving forward.)

SYLVIA: They run.

CLYDE: (Always.)

Silence.

(Sometimes I try—I can dream it away.)

SYLVIA: What?

CLYDE: (Loneliness. The torture.)

SYLVIA: Yeah?

CLYDE: (I dream about so much. More. More than what I have. You think everyone does that?)

SYLVIA: Yes.

CLYDE: (I'm not sure. Not like me.)

SYLVIA: Maybe.

CLYDE: (I live in big houses. I sleep in comfortable beds. I have no doubts. I have no fears. My dreams keep me in bright boxes. No one can touch me there. But—)

SYLVIA: No one?

CLYDE: (How badly I want to be touched.)

SYLVIA *touches* CLYDE's *arm.*

CLYDE: (I seem to be surrounded by all these boxes now. Closed in. But all of them have leaks. Everything is leaking out.)

SYLVIA: Don't be afraid.

CLYDE: (I'm not afraid really. Just sad. Terribly sad. What did I do with my thirty-six years?)

SYLVIA: Enough. You did enough—

CLYDE: Nothing.

SYLVIA: You did what you could—

CLYDE: (Now I'm rotting away—)

SYLVIA: No.

CLYDE: (I want to begin again. Give me some tape and I'll tape up all these boxes. I'll put me back together. I'll

make me new. I'll seal all the colors and days in. I'll fill
the boxes with people. With lovers. With my family.
With all the people I wanted to know. I'll put you
inside with me.)

SYLVIA: No.

CLYDE: (Oh please.)

SYLVIA: That's impossible.

CLYDE: (I'll punch tiny holes in the top. I will. Just for
air. It won't be bad in there with me. It won't be hot. I'll
be fresh. Clean. I'll be everything the boxes promise.)

SYLVIA: I think you should sleep now.

CLYDE: (I'll be a treasure.)

SYLVIA: Sleep.

CLYDE: (A little song.)

SYLVIA: Sleep, Clyde.

CLYDE: (A surprise.)

SYLVIA: Sleep.

CLYDE: (A gift.)

(SYLVIA *rubs* CLYDE's *forehead.*)

CLYDE: (A brand new gift to the world.)

SYLVIA: Please sleep—

CLYDE: If I sleep I'll never wake up.

SYLVIA: You'll dream.

CLYDE: If I sleep, I'll get visitors. I don't like the
visitors. They have such eyes—

SYLVIA: They're your—

CLYDE: If I sleep, I'll be gone.

Silence.

SYLVIA: So go.

CLYDE: I'm not ready.

SYLVIA: Maybe you are—

CLYDE: (I'm not! I can, I can still feel my lips. I can still wait for them to be kissed. How can I go when I am waiting to be kissed?)

SYLVIA *slowly kisses* CLYDE.

CLYDE: (How can I go when I want more?)

SYLVIA *takes off her shirt. Puts* CLYDE's *hand on her breast.*

CLYDE: How can I go when there's all this beauty here?

CLYDE *cries.* SYLVIA *moves his mouth to her breast.*

Day 32

CLYDE *stares at the ceiling.* WILL *stands over him, checks his breathing. He grabs a pillow.*

WILL *stands holding the pillow. He moves closer to* CLYDE's *face.*

CLYDE *turns his head toward him.*

Day 33

MYRA *and* MEL, *with the baby in the pack, stand watching* WILL *do sit-ups.* [WILL *sits on the pillow.*] MYRA *holds flowers.*

WILL: 55. 56. 57. Improves the stomach muscles. You could scrub shirts on my stomach.
He stops. Lifts his shirt.
See?

MYRA: Why would I want to do that?

MEL: How's the man?

WILL: Clyde?

MEL: Yeah.

WILL: Oh. Same I guess.

He starts more sit ups.

60, 61, 62—

MEL: Same?

WILL: I let Sylvia do most of the nursing. I'm just here for support.

MEL: I see.

WILL: We're our own Hospice team. She stays with him hour on end, talking his fucking ear off, I imagine… and I don't know what else, changing his bedpan and wiping his ass maybe…and I wait for him to die.

He quits. Stops his watch

Twenty minutes. Not bad.

MYRA: We were wondering if there was anything we could do.

WILL: Do?

MYRA: Yes. You know. Say some prayers. Bake something. Tell him stories.

WILL: Why?

MYRA: Why not?

WILL: I think we've got it under control.

MEL: We want to show him the baby.

WILL: Why?

MEL: The kid does wonders.

WILL: He's seen the baby before.

MEL: Of course he has. But we thought it might cheer him up.

MYRA: He cheers us up.

MEL: He sure does. Changed our life.

MYRA: From the inside out.

MEL: We have new purpose.

WILL: Uh huh—

MYRA: I've been stretched beyond myself.

MEL: Me too—

WILL: Well, the man's a clear goner. I don't know what good a baby's going to do him now. You two play tennis?

MEL: No.

WILL: Neither of you?

MYRA: No.

WILL: Hmm…I've got a couple of extra hours in the morning and would really like to hit some balls. Drive them down the court.

MYRA: Can't help you.

WILL: Yoga just doesn't do it for me anymore. I need to hit something. Hard.

(MEL *backs away with the baby.*)

MEL: We're going to go inside.

WILL: I'm not going to stop you. But don't blame me if you can't get the stink off you. It's pretty rancid in there.

MYRA: We're prepared.

MEL: We can handle it.

MYRA: We're ready.

(WILL *turns and begins doing push-ups.*)

WILL: I'm just counting the days. 1. 2. 3. 4. 5…

Day 38

CLYDE *sits with the baby against his chest.* MEL *and* MYRA *stand back, barely able to keep it together. Clutching each other.*

CLYDE: Feels like he's purring.

MEL: I, I know.

CLYDE: He smells good.

MYRA: Thank you.

CLYDE: My mother said I smelled good. "Came out a flower", she said. "A gardenia in my arms." (Don't smell me now, mother—)

MYRA: He's a garden.

CLYDE: "You unfolded and took my breast. Smiling all the while. Lips so soft", she said. (Oh dear mother, I did love you—)

MYRA: He's gentle too.

CLYDE: He's so fragile. Am I hurting him?

MYRA: No.

MEL: Of course not. No.

MYRA: He's stronger than you think.

CLYDE: My father dropped me once. He didn't mean to. He just tripped and he lost hold. I wasn't hurt, but he cried for five hours straight. And then he never picked me up again. Never touched me again. (But I knew you loved me, father. I did know that.)

MEL: My father wasn't much for affection either.

MYRA: Nor mine.

CLYDE: I got used to it though. I did. (We developed this way of looking at each other that became, that kind of became a, a, kind of affection. He would smile, or nod, or look away and I knew that he would have put his arm around me right then. If he could. If he could have.) So I'd smile back and let him know that it was alright he didn't touch me. That his approval was good enough. That I'd take that instead. (But, no, how many times did that feel empty? How many times would I have traded that cowardly glance for one of his strong, massive arms around my slumped, thin, shoulders? Would I have been a bigger, a better man…a proud, successful man if he had been able to give me some of that muscle? Just by being closer to those arms, could I have been a brave man? Moved mountains? Saved the world? Cured cancer even?)

MYRA: Parents do what they can.

CLYDE: I suppose. (But why do so many fail their children?)

MEL: They do try.

CLYDE: I know. (And we love them for that. Even when we wish they could have helped us be, be…solid. Steadfast. A million times happier. Learn how to be truly happy. Without a doubt, teach us that one lesson. "Fuck everything else, son. Concentrate on what the hell makes you happy. Focus on what fills that caved-in chest of yours…you know, Clyde, I really don't know what you have against lifting a few weights. It sure couldn't hurt a boy like you.") He sure has a little body, doesn't he?

MEL: Yes—

MYRA: But he's growing fast.

CLYDE: Kind of strange, when you think about it, when you realize it…that we all were *this* once…had this this tiny skin, this tiny body once…and now the one we have is actually the *same* body. Same hands. Same feet. Same bones and gut and—and then it's so quickly gone. Taken. Robbed. What makes it move and reach and run, is gone and it becomes this rambling, lost carcass that is no one's son. (Come and claim me!)

MYRA: You will always be—

CLYDE: Do I depress you?

MEL & MYRA: No, no. Gosh no. Not at all.

CLYDE: I am kind of a downer, aren't I?

MEL & MYRA: No, no. Gosh no. Not at all.

CLYDE: I don't mean to be macabre.

He pushes a smile.

MEL & MYRA: Please. No. Don't worry—.

They push a smile back.

Silence.

CLYDE: I used to play the banjo. (Watched way too much *Hee Haw* as a kid.)

MEL & MYRA: Really?

CLYDE: That's a happy instrument.

MEL & MYRA: Sure.

CLYDE: Goofy, but happy. (I was never cool. Not for one day. I wish I could have been cool. Everyone adores the cool guy—)

MEL & MYRA: Oh yeah.

CLYDE: You think he likes music?

MEL: I know he does.

CLYDE: What kind?

MEL: Oh, well. All kinds.

MYRA: He likes the Blues.

MEL: He likes the Blues best, doesn't he.

MYRA: Uh huh.

CLYDE: Good taste, this kid. Who's his favorite?

MYRA: Well—

MEL: He likes-—

CLYDE: "Don't know why, there's no sun up in the sky, stormy weather...since my babe and me ain't together, seems it's raining all the time..." (Where's Sylvia?)

Silence.

MEL: Clyde?

MYRA: Clyde?

CLYDE: Do you have a name for him yet?

MYRA: No.

MEL: No.

CLYDE: Give him something cool. (Start with the name—)

MEL & MYRA: Hmm.

CLYDE: I was doomed with "Clyde". ("Clint"? Could I have been a "Clint"?)

MEL & MYRA: It's a fine—

CLYDE: Give him something solid. Stone. Metal. Iron. ("Anvil"?)

MYRA: That could get heavy.

CLYDE: Give him something that can't be broken. ("Rubbermade", "Plasticwrap", "Plexiglass"?)

MEL: Sounds a bit cheap.

CLYDE *stops and stares at the baby.*

CLYDE: Give him something that will not end. (If only "Sky" wasn't so overused. The Sixties really did us in with those names, didn't they? The dawning of Aquarius reeked havoc on a whole generation of restless children who are now toting names they wish had been left in their parents' subconscious. Left in the desert. Out of the bong.)

He kisses the baby.

But I think I'd maybe, I'd just call you, Joe. Something simple. Definitely cool. You can do a lot with that name. (And that's not just because I worked in the coffee business. I promise.) You can be more than average. Joe DiMaggio proved that.

The baby cries.

CLYDE: Where's Sylvia?

MEL & MYRA: Sleeping.

CLYDE: I think I need to see her.

MEL & MYRA: Why?

CLYDE: (The boxes are open. But closing in. Higher we step. Up I go.)

Silence.

MEL & MYRA: Clyde?
They reach for the baby.

CLYDE: Is it bright in here? (Don't drop him.)

Day 45

CLYDE *sits up, looking around the stage. His eyes searching something.*

SYLVIA *searches through* Tibetan Book of the Dead, *this time more desperate. Looking for something. Anything.*

CLYDE *lies down.*

There are candles burning around the shrine. [The shrine is bigger. Some of the candles read "HEALTH", some read "PEACE", some read, "PROSPERITY" some read, "ABUNDANCE".]

CLYDE *sits up. Looks. Lies down.*

SYLVIA *puts the book down in defeat. She picks up the Bible, quickly puts it down.*

She lights a candle and adds it to the shrine. The candle reads, "SURRENDER".

She exits.

CLYDE *sits up. Looks around the stage. Lies down.*

CLYDE *sits up. Searches…*

Day 46

WILL *and* SYLVIA *stand arguing on the side of the stage. She holds a tray of tea and lotions and balms. He checks his watch.*

WILL: What's that got to do with me?

SYLVIA: Nothing.

WILL: See.

SYLVIA: You're selfish.

WILL: I've been waiting four hours for you and I'm selfish?

SYLVIA: Yes.

WILL: How's that?

SYLVIA: You've got the world at your feet. And a tan to prove it. Go entertain yourself for the day and come talk to me later.

WILL: I don't want to entertain myself! I don't want to talk to you later. I want to be with you—

SYLVIA: You have a whole lifetime to be with me, don't you?

WILL: Do I?

Silence.

SYLVIA: Of course.

WILL: I've scoured this damn mountain from top to bottom for forty-six fucking days, talked to every boring local person I could, spent hours getting in shape, and now I look like a million bucks. Don't I?

SYLVIA: Sure—

WILL: But you won't touch me—

SYLVIA: You're selfish—

WILL: I've spent days and days filling my goddamn time with ABSOLUTELY NOTHING!

SYLVIA: The liberty of Nothing!

WILL: I'm tired!

SYLVIA: Take a nap! You'll wake up!

WILL: I've napped myself into goddamn oblivion. I'm bored.

SYLVIA: The luxury of Boredom!

WILL: I miss you!

SYLVIA: A man is saying goodbye to his entire life in there and all you can think about is yourself.

WILL: I'm thinking of you—

SYLVIA: If a train was coming down the tracks toward a crowd of innocent people, you'd be more worried that it wasn't going to get to you on schedule.

WILL *stops looking at his watch.*

SYLVIA: That man has got nothing but a shrinking bag of bones and running film of memories to call his own. That's it. His future is odd light, wild stars and, and Void.

WILL: That's not my problem—

SYLVIA: And what is your future?

WILL: You tell me.

SYLVIA: You have one. You have one, don't you?
Leather chairs, squash matches, Sunday brunch, vases
of gerber daisies next to white sheets with me laying
open to you in the middle. Remember that. While that
man dies—
She tries to exit.

WILL: You've never been open to me.

SYLVIA: What?

WILL: The leather chairs have been warmer.

SYLVIA: You think so?

WILL: The minute I was healthy, you were done with
me.

SYLVIA: That's not true—

WILL: There was nothing to fix. Nothing to save.
Nothing that made you feel needed—

SYLVIA: That's not true—

WILL: Powerful.

SYLVIA: No—

WILL: The closer to death, the more aroused you
become, the more hungry you become. You are a kind
of smiling vulture—

SYLVIA: No—

WILL: You shine in the weakness of men.

SYLVIA: Do I?

WILL: You are made Sylvia, in the moment they reach
for you.

SYLVIA: You think so?

WILL: The minute a man asks for your aid, asks you to
kindly pass the water to wet his tongue, kill his thirst,

bandage his heart...you suddenly rise up and state your claim on him. He is yours. And you are his. The flag of his country. He'd die for you...and you become everything that is beautiful that he can hang his hopes and dreams on—

SYLVIA: So?

WILL: Until finally he would cut his own wrists just because he knows you would come suck the blood, then slowly kiss him back to life.

Silence.

I miss death—

SYLVIA: You're alive, aren't you? Still here. Around to complain about—

WILL: Alive and alone. Give me a razor—

SYLVIA: Is it so much to sacrifice a few of your hours, your wealth of comfort, for another man's pain? Is it?—

WILL: Is it so much to ask that my wife touch me?

(SYLVIA *reaches out and grabs* WILL's *crotch.*)

SYLVIA: There.

WILL *reaches for* SYLVIA.

WILL: I want you, Sylvia. Now—

SYLVIA *pulls away.*

SYLVIA: See? You're selfish.

She exits.

Day 47

CLYDE *lay in bed, laughing. He is surrounded by the shrine and candles.*

CLYDE: (Oh dear...yes...I was something....)

Day 48

CLYDE *and* SYLVIA *are laughing together.*

CLYDE: (Lost in the middle of Arkansas with nothing but a stray cat and half a can of R C cola, that was something. Wow. I never thought I'd live through that.)

SYLVIA: Where'd you get the cat?

CLYDE: (He followed me from Tennessee.)

SYLVIA: Why?

CLYDE: (I ate a tuna sandwich in Chattanooga, and he was mine after that. He never would come close enough for me to pet him, but he would keep right at my feet. For miles. I would have gotten more rides along the way if it weren't for him. You'd be amazed how many people have cat allergies are out there. More than you'd suspect.)

SYLVIA: I guess so—

CLYDE: (But you know, some of those nights, when I was young and trying to find a place to land, trying to decide which direction to go, walking for days, years… and I'm not sure the City was the right direction. I'm just not sure about that now. Other than you being there. And some pretty good hot dogs…but back then…when I was younger…when you're lost like that, when there's not much difference between you and some scrawny cat, you do have to believe that there is something that's gonna keep you alive. You just have to believe that something is gonna come along and save you.)

SYLVIA: Like what?

CLYDE: (A cup of coffee. A half a can of cola. Some toddler tossing his lunch out the window without his mother looking.)

SYLVIA: That saved you?

CLYDE: (He looked me in the eye and threw his hamburger right at me. Then his french fries. One by one along the highway. The cat and I shared those… Are you going to save me?)

SYLVIA: No. I'm afraid not—

CLYDE: (I survived two days on that hamburger. I'd shake that kid's hand. If I could. He'd be a teenager now, I guess. Maybe he's out on some highway. Wandering. Sun-burned and scared. Staring at every car that passes—)

SYLVIA: Maybe.

CLYDE: (Oh no! Don't do it, kid! Find a place to rest yourself. Make something of yourself. Stop. Someplace simple. Quiet. Find a girl. Find conviction. In something! Don't accept status quo!…Grow up to be a man. I'm not a man…)

SYLVIA: You are. A fine—

CLYDE: (I'm not! I'm a child still. Look at me—)

SYLVIA: I am—

CLYDE: (I'm a child full of yellow. I am yellow all over. Coward's color. I never believed in anything! Not one thing! Not even coffee! I hate coffee! …Nothing ever rattled my skull with truth. But you. But you. You believe in so many things. You are all conviction, aren't you, Sylvia? All fight and truth—)

SYLVIA: No.

CLYDE: (You are.)

SYLVIA: No, I'm not.

CLYDE: (I've seen it in you. I studied it. I studied you. You are going to teach me. You were going to show me—)

SYLVIA: No.

CLYDE: (Why not? Of course—)

SYLVIA: Words, Clyde. That's it. That's who I am. I live in a glass house.

CLYDE: (No.)

SYLVIA: You, this, this right here…you…this is Absolute. There's nothing more certain than this—

CLYDE: (No. No. This is just yellow. Just like me. Falling out all over the place. Bursting out around me. Where's it going, this color? Why's it so fucking bright? Sickening? Glare. So full of sparks. Let me know where it goes. And ends. And what awaits me in the heat? Who? A great field of sunflowers or or singing canaries or some kind of burning yellow fire that takes me away in one fat and heavy breath? A baby's first gasp? …No! I want to stay and have one more chance to be a man. To be of USE. One more—)

SYLVIA: You've already done it—

CLYDE: (No. I haven't. I never did it. I ran from everything that ever could have held me…I'm dying in the face of my only chance. Loving you would make me a man, see? I know it would—)

SYLVIA: Clyde—

CLYDE: (It would.)
He stands up. Slowly

SYLVIA: I'm sorry, but it wouldn't—

CLYDE: (It would! Because it's TRUE. It's FULL. STRONG. BRAVE. It's UNDENIABLE. It's, it's scraping my bones right now. It's that miserable ecstasy like no other…it's that pulling of my guts down to my feet. I stumble on my lungs. That's me growing up. I feel it—)
He stands. Wobbly, but—

SYLVIA: Clyde, this right here is the bravest thing you'll ever do—

CLYDE: (NO!)

SYLVIA: You're the king of men right now—

CLYDE: (No! I don't want *that* kingdom! It's, it's not my gold! It's too far away! There's nothing I want there!)

SYLVIA: Freedom from everything—

CLYDE: (No…No…I don't want it—)

SYLVIA: Bliss. The ultimate—

CLYDE: (NO! I want—)

SYLVIA: Enlightenment—

CLYDE: (Flesh!)

SYLVIA: Freedom—

CLYDE: (Let me crawl inside you and stay there. Let me crawl inside you and leave before I know what it feels like to come out. Into the cold again. You are the only fire that I want to be burned up inside. Ashes to ashes in you. Don't you see? …Let me leave in your blood. Strong blood, like yours, pumping red. I could wave goodbye in it. I really could—)

SYLVIA: You can't, Clyde. I'm—

CLYDE: (Oh please…Red is the only color I want now. This yellow is too bright and unyielding. Red is, is still full of life, isn't it? Oozing, wasting life? Let me take some of you with me, Okay? Just a bit. A taste. Of blood. Of pure blood. Yours is so very sweet, I'm sure…I could last forever on it. Unafraid. I would feel safe. FULL.)

SYLVIA: Clyde—

CLYDE: (Complete, without a regret, no cares in the world—)

SYLVIA: Clyde—

CLYDE: (Cool man, strong boy, endless, unbreakable hero. You name it. I'll be him. Call me Freedom. Your blood's my path—)

SYLVIA: I can't, Clyde. I'm not who you think I am—

CLYDE: (Red sea—)

SYLVIA: I'm the coward here—

CLYDE: (Parting—)

SYLVIA: I live by proxy. To everything important. Even death—

CLYDE: (Your blood—)

SYLVIA: I'm living on you. I create nothing…but sentences…on top of sentences—

CLYDE *grabs a small knife from the tray of instruments.*

CLYDE: (I'll take it with me and never be thirsty and never be weak and never be lost again..I'll swim in it…whole…it will mix with mine and make me a man and I'll lift a thousand mountains out there and yell a million golden truths and climb a billion steps beyond the sun with your blood pushing in me like Zeus and no one will ever say that a day was wasted in Clyde Macey's life…no…only a moment or two, just to reflect maybe, just to catch a glimpse of a flying bird or to watch a storm cloud passing or maybe a blue moon rising—because he had to stop and watch those things or die of insincerity, die of ingratitude—but little else slipped by him, no, ma'am, because the rest of his time was a Victory, you see…a biographer's dream….a great success for every searching soul out there because he finally found the Truth that filled his bony chest, that made him Happy, the woman who finally showed him LIFE!…oh, God…how I want to start again.)
Silence.

(LET ME START AGAIN!)

Silence. He moves closer to her. He kisses her.

(Let me do it again.)

SYLVIA *guides* CLYDE'*s hand to reach for her. He gently slices her neck.*

First he reaches out and touches the blood with his finger. Tastes it

He then reaches up and grabs her, using all his strength to pull her towards him, and places his lips against her bleeding neck.

He stops, looks at her, smiles.

CLYDE: (I knew it was sweet…warm…ah yes…see… this is why the frightened earth will always circle the sun…looking for a way in…let me in…I say, let me in.) *He presses his lips to her neck for more.*

Day 49

MEL *and* MYRA *walk through the theatre, toward the stage.*

MEL: Just a few more hours. Then we'll come home.

MYRA: But it's too early. I want to hold him. Surely he's ready to—

MEL: No, no. There's more to see. Much more to see.

MYRA: He won't know where I am, where he begins and ends—

MEL: That's okay. That's quite alright. *I'm* going to show him this time—

MYRA: Not even a name, Mel. But… We gotta give him something to hold onto. Anything… How about "John"?—

MEL: "Seymour"?

MYRA: "Simon"?

MEL: "Paul"?

MYRA: "Fred"?

MEL: "Astaire"?

MYRA: No. No. I hate them all. They won't do.

MEL: Insufficient.

MYRA: But we really should give him something—

MEL: He's got you, me, and a thousand trees to hold onto. Let's let him name himself.

MYRA: He won't know how to do that.

MEL: Sure he will. You watch.

MYRA: What if he calls himself something we don't like. Like, like, "Skip"?

MEL: "Skip"?

MYRA: Yeah?

MEL: Well…huh…guess we can't stop that. Can we?

MEL *and* MYRA *make their way up to the stage.*

MYRA: No. I guess not.

MEL: We gotta trust him. Let him make up his own mind.

MYRA: Seems like a lot to put on a kid, Mel.

MEL: He can handle it.

MYRA: I know, but it's just an awful lot—

MEL: You watch. He'll be ready for anything. He'll be solid. Sure.

MYRA: Well, of course. He's my son—

MEL: "Skip", "Charlie", "Tony", "Bill", you name it… he'll be a great man. Man among men.

MYRA: Tall in the saddle—

MEL: Intrepid.

MYRA: Without a doubt—

MEL: He'll know exactly who he is.

MYRA: You're going to do that, Mel? Really do it—

MEL: Full force. Full time. Father. That's me.

SYLVIA *stands smoking in the corner of the stage. Her neck dry with blood.*

MEL: Oh. Morning.

MYRA: Morning.

SYLVIA: Morning.

MEL: How's the man?

MYRA: Clyde.

SYLVIA: Gone.

Silence.

MYRA: For, for the best, I guess.

MEL: Yep…I guess.

Silence.

A collective sigh on the stage.

WILL *enters taping his watch. It's stopped.*

WILL: You spend a thousand fucking dollars on a lifetime guarantee and what does it get you? Squat.
He sees SYLVIA*'s neck.*
What happened?

SYLVIA *touches her neck. Tastes it.*

SYLVIA: I gave blood this morning.

WILL: What?

SYLVIA: He's gone.

WILL *looks her over, confused. Looks behind him. Around the stage. For* CLYDE.

WILL: What time?

MEL: What's it matter, the time?

WILL: Marks it. The end. Period.

SYLVIA *rubs her face, tired.*

MYRA: You alright?

SYLVIA *nods.*

The baby begins to cry.

MEL: Well then…wish we could stay, but the sun is high, the day is new—

WILL: I'm gonna need a new watch—

MEL: This boy has to keep moving. So. Off we go.

MYRA: You'll walk that baby into a man before we know it.

MEL: If he's lucky.

MYRA: What if he calls himself, "Lucky"?

MEL: That's a good name.

MYRA: Seems a bit presumptious. What if he breaks his leg?

MEL: True.

MYRA: God forbid.

MEL *and* MYRA *begin to exit—*

SYLVIA: Can I hold him?

MEL *and* MYRA *stop.*

SYLVIA: Can I hold him? Before you go.

MEL *and* MYRA *look at each other.*

Myra: Of course.

MEL: Of course.

CLYDE'S INNER THOUGHTS *enters.*

He takes the baby from MEL, *and passes him to* SYLVIA.

SYLVIA: Oh my.

END OF PLAY